CW00802848

BRIDGE OF ALL
In Old Photographs

By

J. Malcolm Allan

Dr. W. H. Welsh Educational and Historical Trust
&
Stirling District Libraries
1989

INTRODUCTION

This publication is a joint enterprise of the Dr. W. H. Welsh Educational and Historical Trust and Stirling District Libraries. It complements the text of *Bridge of Allan: the rise of a village* (1970) by Ella Maclean. Her collections, those of her husband Archibald Maclean and of John J. McKay, now in the trust's care, have provided the photographs (except for three) and the information.
The book is dedicated to these three historians and continues their work.

ACKNOWLEDGEMENTS

Andrew Muirhead of Stirling District Libraries has seen the book through the press. Mary McIntyre and Craig Mair, members of the Trust, assisted with the selection of material: research, text and compilation by J. Malcolm Allan.
Bridge of Allan Community Council gave permission for use of the current street map.

Gifts of information and photographs of Bridge of Allan and the parishes of Lecropt and Logie are always welcome to add to the local history collection provided in Bridge of Allan Library by the Trust.

ISBN 1 870542 12 6

Front cover:
The old Bridge
1520-1958

Printed by
Cordfall Limited
Civic House
26 Civic Street
Glasgow G4 9RH
Tel: 332 4640

Rear cover:
Museum Hall no. 2
1847-1905
Museum Hall no. 3
1886

The Bridge and Allanvale Road. This scene, taken from the river in July, 1890 shows almost the same view as on an engraving of 1820, Allanvale Road is shown near the junction with New Street. The natural slope of the river bank has had to be raised for protection. The flow of the Allan Water has changed now that the weirs and mills above the bridge no longer regulate the torrent in spate. Some of the buildings shown still exist unaltered.

3

The Old Bridge of 1520. Photographed in the 1950's from Lovers' Loan looking down to Bridgend. The left hand side shows the Jubilee Path and old men sitting on the wall opposite where the Change House properties were demolished. Across the river and the lade the Bridge Inn and the Meal Mill, remnants of 18th century Inverallan, face Avenue Park and the Keirfield Institute (1908) while behind stretches the new Cawdor Gardens, built in 1948; three stages in the changing face of Bridge of Allan.

Avenue Park, Keirfield. Shown here in 1937 with bunting out to celebrate the Coronation of George VI, these blocks on Inverallan Road resemble mining village rows, but were built for workers' families at the Keirfield Bleach Works in the latter half of last century. Wash-houses and communal toilets were in the centre, with drying greens at either end. They were not demolished until the 1970's.

'Gladstone Square', Keirfield. These cottages, previously thatched and later roofed with sheet iron, stood on Inverallan Road. The float is a coal cart with two pews mounted on it to carry the children of the 'Bridge of Allan Free Church Sabbath School' in a procession to celebrate the Coronation of Edward VII in 1902. The horse is decorated and the children carry Union Jacks to mark the occasion. The usual route for such parades was Keirfield or Station Road, to Melville Place and back by Keir Street.

Keirfield Institute. Pullars, owners of the Keirfield Works, built this reading room and recreation hall at the entrance to the Works at Inverallan Road in 1879; it was one of the few brick buildings in the old village.

Before church halls were built, the Sabbath school met here and social events were so successful that a larger hall was built in 1908 opposite the Bridge Inn next to the Smithy. The tenement to the left was originally a mill.

The Entrance to Keirfield Works. This is now Steuart Road. The old Institute was at the left and the manager's house can be seen beyond the railed corner. The cottages in the foreground, traditional two roomed 'but and bens', were known as 'Chuckie Row' and are thought to have been housing for the bleachfield workers prior to the building of Avenue Park. They were demolished in 1931.

Chuckie Row. A late 1920's view of the cottages from Inverallan Drive corner as the road turns to the Little Carse walk and Lecropt. The view of the village behind is clear to Allanvale Road across the river. Trinity Church stands high in front of Lower Westerton Wood and Mine Wood on the ridge.

From Keirfield Chimney July 1910. This view of Keirfield and Inverallan looking towards the Miln of Airthrey has the chimney of the old Gas Works to the left. The Gas Works functioned from 1840 to 1905; on its demolition in 1919 the stone was re-used for Allan Park Crescent (1922).

Avenue Park and the new Keirfield Institute are at the right with Salisbury Cottage beyond, across the river. Station Road, at that time the main road north, is clearly to be seen, but now Cawdor Road and Inverallan Drive fill the fields up to the station goods yard.

Old White Bridge. The original White Bridge was washed away in 1877; this is the second one, which was washed away in the floods of 1909. Both of the earlier bridges were wooden, but the present White Bridge is iron and was erected in 1910. The bridge was necessary for pedestrians from the workers' cottages on Allanvale Road going to either the Bleach Works, shown in the centre of the picture, or to Keirfield Farm.

Allan Water Flood. The great flood of 18 January 1909, which washed away the White Bridge, marooned the works and manager's house, right, near Chuckie Row, taken from Allanvale Road. This area will be the scene of the latest flood prevention scheme in June 1989 as this book is in the press. Fields further along were known as The Sponge because of regular flooding opposite the allotments.

Station Brae about 1890. Until 1957 this was the main road north. As the tracks of the iron-shod cartwheels show, at the time of the photograph, it was a dirt road. It was only paved with stone blocks in 1913. The white building in the centre was the Smithy, flanked by the Bridge Inn and the Meal Mill; the pantiled building closer to the camera was Inverallan Inn and brewery. In the distance the spire of St. Andrew's Parish Church, now Holy Trinity, rises above the skyline of the village while the Wallace Monument on a treeless Abbey Craig dominates the horizon.

The Station. Horse buses from the Queen's, the Royal and Carmichael's Temperance Hotels line up with a parcel van in the yard of the old Station which functioned from 1848 to 1965 and is now a house. It was built of bricks dug from the Cornton Brickworks, begun in 1845 to provide lining bricks for Dunblane Tunnel. The Brickwork site is now Westerlea Drive and Carsaig Cottages, the latter being the remnants of the Gasworks built on the site in 1905. Bridge of Allan Station was the site of one of the first John Menzies Bookstalls in 1857.

Jardine's House. Dated from around 1700 as a farm house. Until it was demolished in 1945, this was the last of a group of 18th century houses between the Meal Mill and the station. Next to Jardine's House stood Rose Cottage, a heather thatched bothy, which survived until 1933. The site is partly under the new A9 where it is embanked behind Station Road. Two similar houses remained there until Inverallan Court was built round one of them.

Inverallan 1958. The remains of the stone wall of the old bridge, freshly demolished, are behind the outbuildings where the steps lead to the sluice of the mill-lade to Keirfield. The 18th century house on the right is now surrounded by Inverallan Court retirement flats. The Meal Mill in the centre, built around 1710, operated until the 1940's when it became a store. From 1970-78 it was the 'Inverallan Mill', a shop selling Scottish woollen goods. Thereafter the machinery was removed and the building is now offices. The pantiled brewery was demolished to make a car park.

The New Bridge, built 1958. The New Bridge was designed in 1938 but as a result of the war was not built until 1956-58. It was built in two parts so that traffic flow could continue. The steel for the re-inforced concrete came from Poland due to shortages in this country; the granite facings came ready dressed from Aberdeen. The east half opened in 1957, the first vehicle across being a dust-cart. The buildings to the left of the Bridge Inn and to the right of the Meal Mill have now gone.

The Meal Mill. Part of the Mill Lade near the wheel still exists, but the rest is filled in. The meadow where the cows and hens are shown, known as Cameron's Haugh or Hornshaugh, is now divided by the A9. The part in the foreground became Inverallan Road, the riverside remnant a public park.

Beyond the telegraph poles can be seen the chimney and buildings of the paper mill which operated for 200 years up until 1946. The machinery went to Calcutta, the chimney was demolished in 1960 and the surviving buildings became a warehouse.

18

Sunnylaw. Sunnylaw was one of the many separate clachans which were linked up by the new villas within the last century. The first few houses of Blairforkie Drive are centre, with Glen Road above and Darn Walk below. The tiled cottages to the right were at the foot of Ferniebank Brae above the paper mill cottages. The photograph was taken from the original signal box of the old station and shows goods wagons in the bottom corner.

Paper Mill Cottages. Between Blairforkie Drive and the Darn Walk, these pantiled cottages served the old paper mill below which dated from the early 18th century and was pulled down in 1948. The Darn Walk to Dunblane follows the mill lade to the later Airthrey Paper Mill; the sluice walls can be seen near the weir. Among those living in the cottages were a hat-box maker and a millwright. Henhouses stand in the centre of each cottage plot.

Miln of Airthrey Road. Cameron's Haugh on the left is now the park at the riverside. This mill, one of ten mills on the Allan Water, was originally a woollen mill and later a sawmill. It was demolished when the road, now known as **Blairforkie Drive**, was widened and remade in 1909. Salisbury Cottage opposite survived until 1964.

Allanside Cottage, Miln of Airthrey Road. This heather thatched cottage stood at the foot of Paper Mill Brae until 1908. A similar cottage, Rose Cottage, stood beside Jardine's farm and was occupied until 1926. Both were part of the original village housing about 1700. Pantiled cottages of later in the century stood further up Blairforkie Drive. A closet or privy lean-to can be seen at the gable.

Milladd or Black Pete's. Beyond Stevenson's cave a clachan on the Wharry burn included Milladd, marked on a 1783 map as a mill where the Darn Walk reaches Kippenross. A wooden footbridge is still maintained as a result of a Court of Session ruling in 1858. A drove road crossed here to Drumdruills on the way to Pathfoot tryst from the Trossachs, but all dwellings have gone. The entrance to Kippenross for the older Darn Walk along the river bank was walled up.

Airthrey Paper Mill, 1890. The last of several paper mills on the Allan, it is now the entrance to the caravan park. The mill manager's house of 1743, remodeled, is next to the Mill with Milsey Bank, built in 1833, across the river. Wooden baulks divide the weir, and the road is shown as it was before it was cut back and strengthened by a stone retaining bank beside Cosy Cottage gable, where there is now a rose garden and seat.

Blairforkie Drive. The road surface was raised in the improvement of 1909 which cleared away the sawmill, leaving Salisbury Cottage, shown on the left. Excavations for the stone retaining wall by Cosy Cottage revealed a mine addit and a reputed illicit whisky still.

The shop and houses at Bridgend have since gone but the property remains at Inverallan. The new bridge was built in front of the old one shown here. This was the first surfaced road into the village, and the gas lamps mark the beginning of the village.

Bridge-End Houses. From the river at Paip's Linn, the seventeenth century change house was later built up to the road height. The men on the left side sit on the wall of the bridge, above the iron stair going down to the original level. The top floor of the centre three storey building had Cadien's shop, entered from Henderson Street. The lower floors were entered from a lane or pend behind the black and white police station at the corner of Allanvale Road.

Cadien's Shop Bridgend. The same buildings from the main road show only the top floor above the level of the road. The road was raised to make the approach to the old bridge more level. The half timbered gable end is part of the police station shown in the previous photograph. All of this had been taken down by 1950 to straighten the road in preparation for the new bridge.

Police Station 1893-1937. The same building shown from the opposite direction shows the Police Station built on the toll house base. During World War II the Home Guard used the property as its headquarters; Ex R.S.M. Anderson, who was a Black Watch Veteran of the Battle of Tel-el Kabir in 1882, drilled the platoons, who slept in the cells when not on duty. The buildings were also earmarked for use as a mortuary had there been heavy air-raids. The black and white style is the same as the Studio in Union Street. The combined 'Bridge' and 'Double Bend' sign on the left is a reminder of how much the road has been straightened.

Queen's Hotel. A hotel bus which met the trains, stands outside the Queen's Hotel opened in 1839 as Airthrey Wells Inn by a Mr. Barr who was a former steward on the Stirling to Edinburgh steamers. Prior to the coming of the railways in 1848 a horse bus ran five times a day from Stirling.

Opposite, on the right, is Sunnyside built in 1837 as Philp's Inn. In 1842, Philp built the Royal Hotel. In the distance can be seen the white toll house shown in the previous photograph as the base of the police station.

Stirling Road (East) 1885. On a dirt road a delivery cart and barrow stand outside the shop of John Graham, first provost in 1893. The Lady of the Lake Hotel was above it with fancy gas lamp over the door.

Opposite, a boot hangs outside a shoemaker's built at an angle to the old road above. Outside Henderson's a sign reads "Register of visitors and Lodgings to let kept within", this is now the site of the Allan Water Cafe.

West End Cottage. Built 1770, possibly as an inn, this building beside the Allan Water Cafe was demolished in 1950. All the houses beyond were demolished for the present row of shops with flats above. The spire beyond is Trinity Church, 1898-1948, now the Well Road park site. The Lady of the Lake Hotel lamp projects above the car.

Lover's Walk. Part of the old road behind the shops, forked to Lover's Loan leading to Sunnylaw along the side of Westerton House grounds.

Right

Wharry Glen. Another favourite walk to the bridge built by Robert McVicar of Menstrie, a mason in Dunblane from 1808, when the Glen Road to Dunblane was cut in the 1840's.

Lecroft Kirk and The Laird's Loft. Built in 1827 as a 'Laird's Kirk'. The door only entered a sitting room behind the laird's loft until 1964, when stairs were cut through. Stirling of Keir moved the village and school off his estate and demolished the mediæval St. Moroc's church. There had been worship on the site since around 800 a.d. Nothing remains of Lecropt village except the Kirkyard.

Old Lecropt Kirkyard. Now enclosed in the grounds of Keir estate, nothing remains of St. Moroc's except a few stones behind the railing. The gravestones include a table tomb and headstone with a skull and crossed bones.

After demolition in 1827 there was no sign of a community dating back 1000 years and more, where James IV came on pilgrimage. The motorway divides the old kirk from the new.

Westerton House built 1803 c.1880. Sir James E. Alexander and family stand where the Strathallan Games began in 1852, founded by his brother Major John Alexander Henderson. A curling pond, lit by gas lanterns, was on the flat land above. Alexander Drive was part of the old road until 1809 when Stirling Road was made.

Stirling Road is now Henderson Street named after the planner of a new Bridge of Allan and sponsor of the book *A week in Bridge of Allan* (1851). The estate was originally the Wester Toun of Airthrey.

CHINA, CRYSTAL & FANCY WAREHOUSE

BURNS

Mrs. Burns' Shop. Holiday toys include skipping ropes, wooden spades, tennis rackets, wheel barrows, a wicker doll's pram and a drum hung round the door. In the window are toy horses, a bugle, open books, balls, a soldier and a doll. The souvenir china tumblers, vases and ornaments accompany the useful items — teapots, a candlestick and walking sticks. It is a fascinating glimpse of an 1880 shop and is now part of Glenallan Fashion Shop.

The Library c.1890. At least five different Wallace Monument souvenirs are shown with Mauchline ware and china in the right hand window. The reflection is of the first Trinity Church opposite. Erskine published a 200 page guidebook, lists of visitors, arranged letting, and was also a town councillor. The library, hiring books, was at the back of the shop. The windows have gas lighting. The shop is still a newsagents' but no longer hires pianos for visitors to practice or entertain themselves in the evenings.

Opposite

Elmwood. A typical four-square villa with attics; the maid stands at the door, the dog on the step, the canary cage in the window, all ready to welcome guests since the sign over the door reads 'Apartments'. It represents the main service industry of holiday letting on the main North Road. It stood opposite the Queen's Hotel where the new shops are.

Right

Fountain Road. From behind the Royal Hotel the view is of the Post Office and shops which in 1903 replaced the old Music Hall. Formerly called Market Street, until the fountain was put up in 1853, it demonstrates the moving away of the commercial centre from the Bridgend. Behind across the River Forth, Stirling Castle is the viewpoint towards which the villa bay-windows faced.

Old Music Hall. Now the site of the supermarket and post office, this was the social hub as assembly rooms from 1840 for concerts, horticultural shows and lectures. When episcopal church services began in 1854 the secular pictures in the reading room were taken down each Saturday. A wooden building with rustic tree-trunk pillars, its use declined after the Museum Hall was built in 1886. Macdonald's shop is shown at the front with a thermometer and coal merchant's advert. It was demolished in August 1902.

Royal Hotel. Built 1842 as Philp's Hotel on Stirling Road, later Henderson Street. The workmen watched Queen Victoria's visit from the scaffolding. Robert Philp, senior, stands by the gate as Philp's Tartan bus waits in the dirt road. Both Charles Dickens and Robert Louis Stevenson stayed here. It was extended and remodelled several times from the central core.

Henderson Street (West). About 1900 the width of the pavement is noticeable below the hanging bay windows. A boy stands where stone sets have been put in the dirt road so pedestrians could cross dry shod out of the mud in wet weather. Royal Hotel Livery Stables was opposite the hotel and Finsbury Cottage is next to it. The spire of the second Trinity U. P. Church of 1898 was a focal point, almost a pivot of the town.

Stirling Road (West). The 1870 Penzance Buildings, little changed in this 1885 view, was a grand speculative shopping development not continued elsewhere. The first shop, a grocer and wine merchant became the Co-op. The man in white top hat is in front of the Library. A stone drinking fountain was replaced by the Paterson clock in 1898. Across the tram lines can be seen the first U. P. Church of 1849 and Allan Grove, until recently the bank house.

Tram Terminus. Single track horse trams ran from Stirling July 1874-February 1920. A single deck open toastrack ran in summer. The terminus was Well Road and behind the World War I conductress is the first Museum of 1843, which was the Town Council chambers from 1870 to 1939. The museum moved to Coneyhill in 1847 at MacFarlane Terrace. Electrification plans for the trams were cancelled once a rival bus service began in 1919 from Royal Hotel Stables.

Finsbury Cottage. West of the Royal Hotel this was built in 1841 and had a chequered history as a house, Parochial Board offices, a house with carrier's business, Town Clerk's office and finally a petrol station c. 1939. Soon it closed because of petrol rationing during the war and was demolished in 1942. Another purpose-built petrol station opened on the site which is now a car park.

Westerton Arms. About 1900 a lawn tennis party assembled to be photographed from the window of Ramsay's Studio on Union Street. Now the site of a car park and Lodge Abercromby of 1934, it was formerly a bowling green. The Westerton in the background was built as a reading room in 1842 and became a hotel in 1848. Verandas on three sides were supported on tree trunk pillars now built into the walls as the lounge extended. There was a Tennis Club at Mine Road from 1895 and at the municipal court in 1924.

The Studio, Union Street. Built 1888 as a photographic studio and art gallery by Colin Ramsay senior, who also had a studio in Glasgow, it is in the same mock Tudor style as the later police station. By 1921 George Hughes, FRPS, succeeded Ramsay's son and provided many photographs to illustrate town guidebooks. It is now converted to offices. Note the barefoot children — (shoes were for Sunday) — and the bowling green bench.

Drummond Cottage. In 1844 the Free Church was built on the corner of Union Street. After Chalmers Church was built in 1854 it was a school until 1875. A new local school with a playground was then located between Union Street and Fountain Road. The Belfry from the church was re-erected over a garden gate to Fernfield in Melville Place now Holy Trinity Manse garden.

Blackdub Farm c. 1906. With the round haystacks at the left, this farm stood back from Cornton Road. As Strathallan Road and Orchard Road covered some of the fields, and later Strathallan Court, the name Blackdub was turned down as unsuitable. One or two trees from the drive remain opposite the new sports pavilion. The field below was marshy towards Centenary Walk and the ground raised by infilling.

Strathallan Games c. 1910. The corner of Mayne Avenue and Airthrey Avenue, then part of playing fields for Stanley House School, approximates where the gymnasium shed stands. Behind the grandstand of 1889 are the fields of North Cornton Farm where the present primary school is on Pullar Avenue. A curling and skating pond was on the Mayne Avenue area for a few years.

North Corntoun Farm. At the right angle bend where Pullar Avenue now is, it belonged to a younger son of the Earl of Airlie in 1700. It stood between Orchard House (1905) left and the Games Stand (1889) right, surrounded by the 50 acre Scott's Jam Orchards. The Primary School stands on the ridged fruit field and the rest was built over by the Orchard Estate in the 1960's.

Hungry Kerse Cottages. The name indicates poorer crofting and these cottages were also known as The Hen Trap and Cock-ma-lane. Until 1911 they stood between Cornton Road and the river, where Cornton Crescent was built in 1924.

Between these dates it was the Cornton Hutment camp for 1000 troops during World War I. The cottages were very old and primitive and had pantiled roofs.

Blawlowan, Pathfoot. A separate estate of six acres near Airthrey it included an Inn and a Tannery as the road from Sheriffmuir came through the cutting. It supplied leather for the shoemaker village of Pathfoot where the Highland cattle came down to the tryst. Called East Lodge for a while, the centre part of Blawlowan is of 1731, the right is older and formerly thatched. Sheltered by the rock and serviced by a natural burn for the tan pits, it was occupied for 250 years by the Bryce family.

Delivery Cart c.1900. The outlying parts depended on delivery, a service all the shops provided. Private horse buses delivered passengers to the hotels. At stables horses and carriages were for hire. The horse was the main transportation up to World War I with two smithies in the village. Elder, the baker, with a shop also in Dunblane, was proud enough of the new bread cart to record it. The driver sat on the top.

Charabanc Trip 1900. The U. P. Church choir outing parked at the corner of New Street outside Elder's shop, which is still a baker. The small boy is barefoot. The choir nearly all wear straw hats and best clothes which would get dusty from the road. The hanging bay-window in New Street was a regular feature of Bridge of Allan architecture in both wood and stone, so that visitors could see views from their lodgings or watch the street activity below.

Mine Road c.1900. Since 1861 the Airthrey Spa Bowling Club have played on a green laid out in 1840 by a Mr. Barclay. He was a lessee of the hotel which was in the Mine House shown on the right. The building was originally erected c. 1738 as dwellings and workshops for the copper mine in the wood. Abercromby Drive was made in 1820 as Spa Terrace looking down to the Wells. The rustic club-house was replaced by the present one in 1924.

Spa Pump Room. A wooden Wells House of 1820 was replaced in 1856 by a stone pumproom with porch and verandah dated 1861, erected by Lord Abercromby. Open from 6.00 a.m. to dusk it was run by the Airthrey Estate until 1893. In 1930 the town council bought the company and built the semi-circular Sun Lounge which was leased to the Allan Water Hotel. The former Hydropathic is now flats; the spa closed in 1946 and is now a restaurant.

Allan Water Hotel. Built in 1864 as Ochil Park Hydropathic Institution to exploit the benefits of the mineral waters, from 1893 until converted to flats it was Allan Water Hotel. The kitchen gardens and pleasure grounds with heather thatch gazebo are covered now by Allanwood Court. Spa buildings are at the left and the Wallace Monument stands on the skyline above Chalton Road villas.

From Drumbrae Farm. The new Victorian town of the 1880's marched east both on flat carse land and uphill terrace ground. Chalton Road and Westerton Drive can be seen, left, with Spa and Hydro at the right. The old village sheltered below the hill at the river pinpointing communication routes and survival resources, surrounded by farms, until the growing popularity of mineral water and the railway accelerated the changes.

Chalmers Church. Several market gardens, some with stalls or shops, occupied the land in the centre of the village before it was built over, in this case by the Royal Bank of Scotland and Chalmers' Church new hall. At the left the shop is now part of Abbeyfield House after a long time as Park Guest House and restaurant. The church of 1854 and hall of 1890 mark the height of the Victorian independence and prosperity, and the break from the estate church and laird's hall, as the village moved east.

Coneyhill / Old Manor. Built as the house for the small Coneyhill Estate c.1766, the old wing was thatched. As Ivy Lodge it had been extended by John Macfarlane in 1849 with a carriage porch and side wing. A new Coneyhill House (1863) is behind on the left with East Hill, his last home, on the right. This was feued from the pleasure gardens and glen of the Red Burn which had fed a small distillery until the early 19th century.

From Cornton to Dumyat. Blackdub Farm, centre, faces a water meadow with cows. In winter it was flooded for a curling pond named Loch Dubh. Behind on the hill is the old Museum Hall at Macfarlane Terrace, off Coneyhill, and fields of Drumbrae Farm clear to Dumyat at the right above Hermitage Wood. Only a few houses are built on Westerton Drive and villas or private schools on Kenilworth Road. The approach and view from Cornton along the rivers was the older and more direct route from Stirling.

Airthrey and Sheriffmuir. At the eastern edge of the encroaching village Airthrey Castle, an Adam design, sits below Hermitage Wood and the rising hills. In the trees is old Logie, in the foreground Airthrey Loch and the fields where the old counties of Stirling, Perth and Clackmannan met. The oldest sign of habitation, the Pathfoot megalith where the tryst was held, is beside the newest development, Stirling University. Encompassed in the one picture is the progression of the community from its origins to the present.

Wallace Monument. Built 1861-1869 on Abbey Craig, to commemorate the patriot William Wallace and the Battle of Stirling Bridge in 1297, the tower looks down to Logie Parish Kirk and Airthrey estate, and up to Dumyat at the end of the Ochils. From here the causeway stretched to Stirling Bridge over the Forth into which Allan Water flows near Cornton. The earliest inhabitants of what was to become Bridge of Allan lived in this area between the rivers and the hills.